ALL OF THIS IS OURS

ALL OF THIS IS OURS

Poems by

Bruce McCandless III

Cover design by Shay Culligan

ISBN: 978-1-954353-44-2

Kelsay Books
502 South 1040 East, A-119
American Fork, Utah, 84003

For Bernice Doyle McCandless

The fire in our winter cabin
The sun on our summer pond
The words of our morning prayer
The notes of our evening song

Acknowledgments

Many thanks to the publications in which versions of the following poems have appeared, occasionally with different titles:

Asphodel: "Baz"
Bayou: "The Hook-Up"
Front Range Review: "Bad Yoga," "Consolations"
Grand Little Things: "Seasons," "Ghosts"
Natural Bridge: "It's Not That I Mind"
Nebo: "Fulton Street," "Resistance," "Breaking"
New Delta Review: "Six Years Gone"
Parks & Points Online Poetry Series: "Snakes"
Pinyon Poems: "Wish We Were There"
Pleiades: "The Hard Sell"
Poem: "Bachelor's Song"
Re:Al: "Morning in Jerusalem"
Seattle Review: "Among Fifth Graders"
Slant: "Their Contract"
Steam Ticket: "Lettered in Poetry"
The Concho River Review: "Two Styles of Devotion"
The Lumiere Review: "Quarantine Days," "Managed Care Jesus"
Utter: "37"

Contents

Homilies

Lamentations

The Hard Sell

The two they sent to see me didn't
bother to knock. Their shirts smelled of sweat.
One had forgotten his belt.
We sat in that room at the front of the house and went over terms.
The redhead played Bad Cop, said
I know you've heard the pitch before.
I said, *So maybe I like to look at your scars.*
He told me if I stayed it would be more of the same:
transmission problems on major freeways; bad timing
in real estate matters; catastrophes visible to no one but me.
The other guy, the one with the glasses,
            occasionally surrendered a smile.
I scanned his blank brochures, had a look at the ads.
All this, I said, tapping my temple.
You can make the arrangements?
He nodded, drained my glass.
This was afternoon. All afternoon.
The night waited just outside my window, trying
to figure which way I was leaning.
Speculation ran rampant. Certain trees bet against me.
I could hear the walls whispering
Take the deal, take it,
knew that I was getting close.

Fulton Street

Live oak trees crack sidewalks over their knees.
You stop, look up, swear you see her in cars
twelve times but never do. You walk the streets
until you're Kerouac again, nearly
all that you imagine, only coughing on exhaust.
Basketball players pirouette as you pass.
No one else seems to see how the sun sears the grass,
or cares to see. And you try to stay lost,
but buses run. Kids laugh, and fall, and yawn.
Bright calendars advertise beer and dead saints.
The prophets were here, but you can't read the paint.
You numbered your days by her. She is gone.
The streets seem to swim in the heat, but persist.
Say still, there is this. *What you had.* You insist.

Foot Soldiers

A clammy day in March we
lifted off from Bergstrom Airport, each of us
carrying our own soft cargo of flesh and lactic acid
like an emissary from our ancestors. The flight was mostly men.
We wore suits from Dillard's. Six-pound shoes.
Off to tend to summary judgment motions and
group investment plans, we kept ourselves to ourselves
till the plane fell through some sky trapdoor and
cans of tomato juice rolled for the exits. It got rougher, too.
We spent those seven minutes of mortality trying not to stare at
each other, not even to speak—just to
hold our random sentences with dignity,
like a kind of instant tumor. All the time I wanted to shout,
Does anyone else realize we're miles above the nearest freeway?
That if this air won't act its age they'll have to call experts to
            figure out who we were?
That we're turbines away from a gymnasium floor,
with numbers tied to what were our toes?
What is God thinking? Are we all just parts of a larger brain?
Will I be forgiven? Who makes mud? Can I hug you?
Till the atmosphere unclenched and everyone
began to look around. I even saw uncertain smiles
before the whole gray group returned again to print-out sheets,
to blueprints, grant forms, and secured transactions.
All matters of the greatest urgency, of course,
and by the time we reached Hobby I had almost forgotten
this brief experiment in communal dread.
I stepped out in the rain, smelled cigarettes and oil
and hustled to grab the nearest cab.
I was beaten by a fellow near-death pilgrim who said
Sorry, pal. I got here first and
shut the goddamned door.

Bad Yoga

My late friend Bill refused
to call it anything but "stretching,"
as in the ninth grade football days when
we'd find a spot on the 40 between the fire ant beds and
do some cherry-picking to get warmed up.
As the sweat pooled beneath our shoulder pads,
tiny reservoirs of fear and regret,
we'd contemplate the royal ass-kicking to come:
screaming coaches, flying spittle, scrambling for the errant pigskin.

      There's no screaming in yoga.

In every class I've been to, music leaks from
obliquely mounted but expensive speakers.
There's an air of elaborate calm, and people talk in
voices so earnest you can almost see quotation marks.
We're doing well, we hear.
The world's an illusion, though
the multi-class prepayment option isn't and
we're our own harshest critics when
what we really need is to be praised to within an inch of our lives.
Our instructor assumes a corpse-based pose. *Shavasana,* she says.
We replicate her mini-death and she nods patiently,
tells us *Just Let Go.* But even now, these decades later,
I see cracked-lipped Coach Finnegan just beyond my face
screaming NEVER LET GO
when you've got A HOLT OF A MAN
you GOTTA BRING HIM DOWN.
Surely that world is dust: a dozen bad-eyed memories,
scars on my knees and the backs of my hands.
The honeyed hum of Krystal tells me not to bother
watching anyone else. And yet I do.
Dude to my right is breathing just a little too hard.
It's clear he thinks he can hold this Downward Dog

downwarder and doggeder than me,
clear as well he thinks he's proving something this way.
I don't know what. I don't know how,
only that it doesn't matter as
we rise up from the sweaty floor in tandem,
exchange appraising glances, now make the shift to
Warrior One.

Big Day

In December you finally get the divorce.
The world's underwater. It's forty degrees.
Autumn has stolen the leaves from the trees.
The city stands painted in shades of remorse.
Through armored doors, past the x-ray machine,
you make your way to Judge Covington's court.
Today she'll preside over those of your sort.
You tell yourself that you won't make a scene.
The judge asks questions, but she doesn't get far.
Your last several answers are meaningless sounds.
Embarrassed, the court reporter looks down
as the bailiff offers to call you a car.
There's really no way to soft-pedal the case
or to wish yourself anywhere else but this place.

After Divorce

For several months I am parallel men:
one living present tense, one right beside
in some illusory world, still with my bride
and screwing things up all over again.
I see a hundred fights I could have fixed,
could *still* fix, maybe, given one more chance.
And so I learn the supplicant's slow dance,
its languid rhythms, its self-aimed kicks.
I think about you while I'm driving home
or leaving home, address you *sotto voce*
to catalogue the ways I miss you most,
as if the rear view was a telephone.
Till one day I see that it's useless to speak,
and in April it rains, week after week.

Killing the Hero

He had to go.
He was always looking elsewhere
while I tried to balance the checkbook.
He was a creature of sudden fierce longings but
no settled habits; a man who couldn't be trusted with money
because he would *spend* it: on motorcycle parts and rubber rafts,
zip lines and ammo and various types of processed meat.
He'd rise roaring from the pool to chase the kids and
end up at a local creek, stalking the shallows for monster larvae.
What are you doing? I'd ask, and he'd answer
I'm saving the world, and everything in it.
That's not a monster, I'd say. *It looks like a crawfish.*
He wouldn't listen. Never did. He had no bed time.
He swore he saw in clouds on the horizon foreign cities,
and minarets, or ziggurats, while the closets
cried out for modular shelving.
So I smothered him. I made him take a position
processing claims for a title insurer—
requesting documents; following through on the checklist.
Slowly he grew timid; shrank from sunlight;
ate his sandwich at his desk.
I thought he would resist but he kept at it till the end,
apparently unaware that he'd been fleeced.
He grew more interested in washing the Crock-Pot
than in chasing the wind to God-knows-where and
one night I put a pillow to his face
(two pillows, actually—that he'd picked out himself) and
draped myself across them till his struggles ceased.
I wasn't sorry. I went to check the doors were locked.
I slept for as long as I could.

Freeze

They say pure water's tough to freeze
It lacks some germ to start within
And I'm no lover of disease,
But this, I think, is use for sin—

To call man to forget first faith
Compel him feed on filth of earth
To leaven every hope with hate
The pure with passion in rebirth

I cannot hold this thing we kill
I know your envy—you, my lies
To save ourselves from drifting still
I curse you, waiting. Close my eyes.

Coda

face it we all
spend nights praying over ourselves
have brains that breed shadows that's how
we touch it sometimes
we see how it is that
we our special treasures
god's favorite gift to god
are burning like thin paper
or are falling from a plane
while we look elsewhere
wham the movie suddenly speeds up and
then the *thank you folks hey*
thanks for coming no
one needs a bulletin just
to tell him what we've seen, I mean
it's in the stillness after every rain
the breath of a lover at four a.m.
her face as blank as a marble floor
tonight the snow's falling
without making a sound
that's what tells us *that's*
what tells us we are
headlines printed three days late
town criers in an injured city
that has already heard
the news

Aversion

Since you left, I've simplified my life.
There's to be no more leaving the house.
Also out: dinners involving more than four ingredients;
difficult—by which I mean non-animated—films;
making my bed; choosing fresh socks.
I would much rather sit just about…*here,* I suppose,
braiding the hair of several unsent letters till they're perfect again,
and the day is safely sandwich-wrapped.
Sure it's unproductive. I know it's a mercy
the nation was never governed by anyone like me, that
we'd still be working on the wording of the Sixth Amendment—
just tweaking it, maybe—and the railroads would remain unbuilt
on account of my plan to lay those tracks on a transcontinental grid
reproducing the layout of Dante's inferno
would probably have taken a hell of a lot of
wrangling over real estate.
Thank God wars happen. Disasters drop by,
return old sweaters, talk about moving to Denver.
Bugs crawl out of themselves and
leave their skins like old opinions.
Otherwise I might be sitting here four years from now,
still recalling the stars of sweat in the crook of your neck,
debating the placement of one last *tumid,* or possibly *insidious,* and
rearranging my closet instead of falling headfirst
to my own redeployment as earth admits its mistakes,
moves on with the story.

Seasons

In August he prayed for October, for
relief from the undershirt stuck to his skin

come October he wished it was cooler
wanted snow on black rooftops but when

December deepened he longed for reprieve
from the darkness descending at four

wanted, in April, firefly evenings
that lingered for hours, wanted

whatever was coming, wanted then
had it and found himself wanting again

Six Years Gone

Last week's blizzard still haunts West End Avenue:
the dog shit snow, the dirty ice.
Supposed to go down to 17 tonight but
I'll dream screened-in porches,
feel Austin's dashboard-cracking heat and hear, in the oaks,
cicadas revving up for a run at the title.
Those days it was always August.
We told ourselves we'd find
that intellectually challenging job first thing
tomorrow. Mornings we watched
hummingbirds attach themselves
like ornaments to the mountain laurel.
The peonies spread purple legs.
It was a perfect world for tortillas.

Now you write to tell me just how little work there is.
The house needs paint, but no one's hiring landscapers.
I send, as always, empty cans.
Does it help receiving my regrets?
(See package under separate cover.)
Once again, you've worn me out. One afternoon
you stumbled home from some fresh war with clueless clients,
wished to God we owned a gun and
hacked at a handful of peppers. Beer bottles later
the music stopped, the anger ebbed.
I took you on my chest, my chin,
your pulse a dolphin beneath
the sea of your skin.

Good times. Big finish.
I will not write again.

Lettered in Poetry

Only four of us lettered in poetry my senior year.
One dude learned a marketable skill in wood shop
and was immediately dismissed from the team.
My prom date stole a hot air balloon and left to join the Rockettes,
or possibly the U.S. Marines but
we were awesome anyway.
We rolled through District 20 4-A like a summer typhoon:
crushed Deer Park's Cowboy Minstrels,
Pasadena's Futurist Ranters, Pearland's Symbolist Bulldogs.
We couldn't do anything right. It seemed to work.
We bled regrets. We screamed till no one could hear us.
We practiced our craft in parking lots,
in sleeping bags on Christmas beaches with impossible bra straps
and in phenomenal middle-aged liquor cabinets.
We rolled naked through cigarette butts and daiquiri mix,
curled ourselves around locker-room toilets,
ran from linebackers, peed in the weight room.
We drilled incessantly: *Metaphor, Simile, Synecdoche, Trope!*
Regionals were another matter: Kashmere had some pint-sized
Amiri Baraka who stunned us with loose-limbed invective
baked in summer heat, as godawful heavy as history itself.
We fired back with haikus soft as primrose petals,
drooped impressively, begged for forgiveness,
quickly forgot when the scores were announced.
Then State: some school we'd never heard of.
That no one had heard of! It ceased to exist in 1974.
They didn't write their poems, they *were* poems,
were songs of dust and empty stores.
I suppose they deserved it. Everything they got.
The vacant lots. The haunted Wal-Mart.
But I still have my trophy, the 2nd Place cup,
that shattered heart beneath a heavy boot,

and evenings when I drive by the school to
observe the kids we redeemed with our sorrows
I wonder aloud if this year, finally,
they'll turn out to cheer for the luckless bastards
who made the team.

Fever Dreams

Requiem

Dawn was content to let itself in like
A teenager home from a very late date
The oceans rarely looked up from their work but
You could watch hawks hover high
Over long flat fields, and storms in three different counties
Were visible like holes in the sky had opened up
To let the rain drain in from a reservoir above
Once on the Nantahala I saw maple leaves the color of brick
Sliding beneath me, perfect in their
Cold museum, all the rocks on their knees,
Spangled shallows stabbed by sunshine
And mica glittering like galaxies in the sand
There were nights in October when moonlight
Pooled in people's yards, filtered into their bedrooms
So they dreamt of voyaging on a dark-shored sea
As the clouds crawled by like whispers
I am not talking about something you could sell
I am just telling you, this is how it was in those days
When the night sky softened in the east
The cut grass called like rough perfume
And at five o'clock the first bird sang

Greetings from Your Ministry of Poetry and Indecision

People wonder what I've been up to since my last publication
in that Kiwanis Club newsletter three years ago and
I don't mind saying in 2019
I named myself to an important governmental post
that didn't actually exist and had trouble getting into my office
possibly due to hopelessly outmoded private property notions
still in effect in parts of our nation's capital
(note to self: *Eliminate Outmoded Private Property Notions)* but
still I issued edicts, largely ignored, for example
ordering airdrops of haiku over central Oklahoma
in hopes of encouraging increased tanka yields,
      or *inwardness* maybe
I admit it might have been hard to tell if it worked
next up: taking positive steps to make American industry
      less efficient
fact is, we've lost fourteen percent of our gross national
      pipe dreams—
fewer accountants are disrobing at their desks during lunchtime
while the boss is locked in the server room with wild hogs
the number of dentists reviving long-lost baseball careers is down
grown men don't dream about what their kids can have
      that they never had;
don't plan space vacations, wish to be pirates,
envision themselves wearing purple tights and utility belts
we're in danger of losing our ability to slack off,
one of the principal factors that made us world leaders
      in dragging ass,
gathering wool, catching some zees, hanging around
look at us now: hyper-caffeinated arugula munchers
what ever happened to the National Slouch?
why don't we peer anymore through curtains of nicotine haze

or stare into cooling cups of midnight
as the elevated rumbles through the night outside?
if Latvia continue to prosper, who'll be left to lie around?
we'll be a world full of Germans, without the vacations
well not if this public servant has anything to do with it
and probably he doesn't but nevertheless
I have laid out a forty-six step plan to revive the trial by fire and
certain medieval disciplinary rituals, including branding
  (the new tattoo!)
and sabotage of all machinery powered by anything
  other than oxen
my handpicked team of petty thieves and organists
is testing ways to further decrease preparedness
  for weather-related disasters,
to add long and completely unnecessary detours to
  the nation's highways
and to bring back a variety of bodily odors
  nearly lost to modernity
we seek tax cuts for the proprietors of drive-in movies
and any business called "Empire of Muffins"
we have increased the transmission of Fox news into outer space
in hopes of scaring hostile invasion forces
straight back to Arcturus and
propose institution of a wigwag-based national security alert
with seventeen signals and some capable of meaning
  only one thing,
like CAUTION: KARDASHIANS PLANNING RELEASE OF
  JONI MITCHELL COVER ALBUM
we are attempting to consult with the Pentagon
on the use of fricatives and the phase-in of
slightly more descriptive military campaign names like
OPERATION TRY NOT TO KILL ANY KIDS WITH THAT

BOMB YOU JUST DROPPED

oh yes we in the Ministry of Poetry and Indecision are out here
   working for you
zigging where we're supposed to zag
spreading truth where falsehood rules,
telling outright lies when the truth starts trusting itself
and if you want to do some one small thing to help, it's
don't tell them that you saw us here or for God's sake
where we'll turn up next

Two Styles of Devotion

Another Sunday at eleven a.m.
we listen to our earnest rector read
selections from St. Luke.
He says, *Who loves his life shall lose it* and
we all say Amen.
We bow to the cross.
After we have sipped the blood of Jesus,
grateful for his sacrifice,
we file back to find our pews, lift
voices to our shoulder blades.

Elsewhere a man hangs
upside down in a green cold creek,
his kayak motionless above him
like the stone on a personal crypt
as he worships the air
and has no time to feel embarrassed for
the poison of his panic
as he struggles
to roll the rock off.

Among Fifth Graders

Like you I held my M.Ed. as if it was a new vaccine
and pledged to the ghost of D.T. Suzuki
that violence would find no foothold *here*.
In my classroom all break times would be silent, and
every child would learn to share.
Three years later I'm getting married—off to law school—
sinking like a stone toward my life. Here's everything I know:
At this age, the boys resemble their mothers.
Grammar will not hold them long.
Stick to pirates and chocolate, and be prepared for comments.
Your students will speculate on just how old your best shoes are.
Some will cheat because they like to.
Mostly they've caught on to cars and
can catalogue the major credit cards but
even your most jaded ten-year-old will sometimes hop like a toad.
In times of crisis, laugh. Scream. Repeat as needed.
Don't stay seated. Roam.
Love Dubstep one day, Merle Haggard the next,
and offer explanations only when nobody asks.
Turn your head when several of your students dance.
Resist the urge to do your own.
Most of all, be strict. Adopt no boy.
Remember June is only *Where the Red Fern Grows* away and
you will never see your favorite kid again
as you see him today, adrift at your desk,
attempting to staple his lips together or handing you
a D-Day drawing—coarse, unfinished—that you will call
(especially those burning tanks)
the best you've ever seen.

The Hook-Up

I finally approached her one night in November,
speaking almost as James Earl Jones as I planned.
I said, *I suppose you've been waiting here, kestrel-eyed, leery,*
for someone to help you exhume what you've lost;
mourning perversely for the death of last Tuesday,
perspiring in wonder at worlds gone for weeks.
The night in such cases might be said to befriend you,
burr oak leaves to listen, and sigh in assent.

      Wrong, she affirmed.
I've been here since nine, but my
strongest desires are cousin to colors.
Also I frequently dream about mud.
There's a bayou, for instance, where I used to swim.
I would want to be held there,
robbed of my breath by my laughter and him,
stoned by the sun as soft banks tumble in.

In the ensuing silence I heard shot glasses clink.
Some jerk on a cell phone was watching, and winked.
I said, *Let's start over.*
You're frankly enchanted by the sway of seed grasses.
You've been known to dance sideways in honor of sunrise,
Grow giddy whenever your feet touch the Gulf, and

                        you, she continued,
are imprisoned by photographs plucked from the gutter,
by regrets for no reason but possessed of long half-lives,
by blueprints of airplanes that never quite flew and
the thought of what Rimbaud or Villon might do,
unstuck in time, left in your place or mine.

I was afraid she might turn to me, empty, sarcastic,
just another wrong turn with a face full of piercings and
cantos tattooed on the small of her back.
When the music eddied, we left oversized tips.
I surveyed her eyes: figured Janis,
Ulysses, maybe Madame Blavatsky.
As we walked 35th Street, she shouted her name.

Breaking

Remembrance held my hands to him today.
I who pulled him, late and killing, free
and covered him, and coaxed down bottled milk
felt for these things. He felt and fought at me

and I had lost him. I will not still again
my colt's quick heart, or mornings let him hide
behind me from grackles, stray cats, or the cold.
Now ribs like surf-packed sand ridge his side.

The splay of hooves I helped has gathered tight,
pulled taut by the surge of his shoulder. He strains
an imperative strength against nothing.
He has never been tested by twitch or by rein,

would not be now if his quick stride held less
contempt for me. He trembles, stares, incensed,
and screams to split the air itself. The mares
stare back. He braces, bolts from fence to fence,

and entering I try him, try myself:
I measure close the steps to where he stands.
He turns and starts toward me—starts, reels back
amazed. Now sees, now feels these hardened hands.

Snakes

One thing's sure,
people seldom see a snake but stop to watch
for several seconds as it
angles off into the underbrush, like
an arrow that barely missed.

Mostly this is misperception.
Snakes try to stay out of our way.
But we want portents.
And so on August evenings
when the air is calm,
a moccasin or a banded water snake
will cross the lake
the only way it can as we
count loose omegas
on the mirrored surface,
mouth a prayer
until it disappears.

Diana Wingate Looks Back

You came like rain, like rain would leave: we make
such deaths our truths. Umbrellas, too, are used
and I observed the way you tried, amused
to let you keep it up till Stacy Park,
my usual stop. You said you wanted my name.
I hadn't, then, dropped it with everything else
as I fought you to board the dry bus? Self-
taught, I refrained from repeating the same
and walked home watching clouds tumble by.
Weeds grew fast in the garden next door.
Two cats hid under a car. By four the storm
had spent itself, and left an empty sky.

Their Contract

Earth barged into the publicist's office, said:
"Nice paneling, pal. I've knocked 'em dead in every known venue,
I've brought down whole blocks of houses and still I'm losing my
      public."
She smiled her best sweet-and-lonely, lit an American beech.
"I need the best press you can get me. I need you to plant
punchy descriptions of redolent mud,
short ululations on my rock undulations and
sonnets to ripening squash."

The PR guy sniffed.
He thought he smelled compost. He wondered how compost
could get to the seventeenth floor.

      Earth continued: "Hey genius, take a note.
I was born five billion years ago but
let's round down. We'll make it four. I spat, I spewed,
I danced like a rocket sealed in a bottle and
oceans pooled as I slowly cooled.
Stage fright, maybe. Rain condensed on the blue curve of space.
The sky itself wept to see my debut."

The seventeenth floor!
The publicist had simply opened a window.
The sky seemed near enough to swim in now.
Cedar elms played fire brigade,
heaving buckets of wind to each other.

      "Experience? Sugar, the word's too small.
Remember the St. Helen's Stomp? The Lisbon Limbo?
And that first step, when everyone cringes and chuckles,
when a dizzy foal falls like a lopsided hayrick? I invented that
      step!

I'm the original goddamned bearded lady,
dripping forests from every jowl.
I'm a dandelion juggler, a hurler of ice knives,
I'm a sabretooth tiger *and* the tattooed lady. Jesus, Sam,
tell 'em how I ingest skeletal form—swallow swords the size of
       trees and
breathe fire through a thousand throats.
I'm tired of working the cable news, druidical love fests,
the occasional blockbuster kill 'em all flick.
I want to be booked at Rotary luncheons somewhere in Nebraska,
at commencement festivities across the Deep South,
bar mitzvahs in Boise, May Days in Moscow.
I beg, I shriek, I blush, I shrink, I sing wind songs,
I dance sea storms, all for—what? Not a hall in Tuskegee?
Not a call, not a mall, not a mid-market morning show deep in
       Missouri?
I'm telling you, I've seen the big stars come and go,
but this is *meshuggeneh,* this is…"

He felt the warm wind and envisioned vacations.
So he shut the window, went back to his work till years later he,
the PR guy, entered Earth's office, and
the frowsy old diva had at him again.
Earth shut the windows. But Earth bore no grudges.
She wriggled out of her gown, bowed from the waist,
was happy to show him all over again
exactly what she could do.

Quarantine Days

Here, a week of rain gave way
to 85 degrees and empty afternoons.
The sun sprawled in a hammock over Austin
and reminisced about Hall & Oates to girls laying out,
which is what people used to do before their social media feeds
like, completely *blew up,* while neighbors
sat in haphazard crescents in the shade of porches
and lobbed greetings at the street.
There was some confusion about what to do next.
A tendril of jasmine peeked through the pavement on Redbud
        Trail,
looked around, and decided to stay. This was Day 6.
On the 15th afternoon NASA detected
daydreams hovering over major cities, one more sign of
threats to the nation's brood supply,
our extensive network of paranoia and fretting.
Pollution was down but lassitude was going nowhere, and
there was serious concern for the bathmat industry,
for our packaged cheese processors, for
the manufacturers of protein powders and to-go meals.
Construction workers pulled pickup trucks over
to the side of Highway 71 and let their dogs drive.
Bicyclists appeared like mayflies, almost as numerous as the virus
        itself.
The skies were so clear I could see reasons for a choice I made
four months ago, and on Day 27
someone planted pumpkin seeds in my front yard.
Security footage indicates the culprit was me.
A retired lawyer disappeared into his library and didn't come back.
They say the books were unruly, hadn't been handled for years,
and when they're in packs like that, well…Everywhere
there were open assignations, random meetings, afternoon strolls.

A woman talked to her ex-husband the following week
but had no ulterior motive. We forgot to note it.
On the 34th, someone emailed the mayor to complain about the
        quiet.
People wondered what to call that flower that looks like a wimple.
Mockingbirds acknowledged that people were listening again and
stopped being quite so argumentative. One was about to be famous
        when,
on the 59th day, the lock-down was lifted. The city put on shoes.
The syrupy songs of warblers faded into the background
as we stepped into the world, heavy with sleep but
hustling to catch up, to make strides, to
shove the nearest rock back up
a highly recommended slope.

Ghosts

You came before we'd practiced what to do,
our late-life accident, our only child.
How could you comprehend our fears for you?

A partial list of things you strayed into:
The neighbors' yard—their porch—the yards beside.
You ran and always we ran after you.

Our sense of dread dug deeper than you knew.
We catalogued your every cough and sigh,
and seldom slept a whole night through.

It sounds ridiculous, and yet it's true
that when you hurt yourself, your mother cried.
How can I count up all her tears for you?

We hoped it was some passing interlude,
the way your sorrows made us ache inside.
How can you understand our fears for you,

or know the waking dreams you've led us through?
You've been our joy, our death, our breath, our pride
so long that when you leave, you'll leave us to
the thousand injured ghosts we raised with you.

Resistance

Consider the tyranny of light.
It occupies all the main streets.
Night lives on small reservations.
The stars beat a hasty retreat.

We are never away from our noise:
from our infinite amplified kings.
Thin voices shriek from the static,
emphatic, not saying a thing.

A thousand sentinel streetlights
surround the steel cities again.
Somewhere under cover of darkness
a man weeps with the joy of his sin.

He whispers these words to his lover,
decrescendo of blood warming bone,
One day they will come for our shadows.
We must hide every evening we own.

Bachelor's Song

I count red lights on the Westlake towers,
watch frantic leotards dance on TV.
I'm glad I decided not to send flowers.
I stare into cigarettes, stir cups of tea.

I spend my weekends avoiding all crowds.
I need to reflect—to read, maybe rest.
It's important to sit and try thinking aloud.
It's these Saturday nights eating fruit I like best.

McKay in Accounting insists that he's right.
He burbles of being best friends with his wife.
I recall the touch of your lips, try to fight
your plots to change my perfect life.

Homilies

To A Friend, On His Wedding Day

You watch her as she walks the aisle and
swear to God you'll never go—
as if your words could make it so. Truth is,
all men hunger all the time for comely interns; accolades;
for flying lessons and foreign cars.
Every average morning's another arrow—one more proof
you'll leave no legend. You pluck it out.
By the time you hit the Kirkwood Exit you've
outwitted Osama, captured a pirate,
stopped somewhere west of Laramie
the senseless bullying of ministers and aging dogs.
At work you storm whole ranks of mortgage banks,
fight for provinces of ergonomic chairs.
Achievement almost ends it. But does not.
Consider Alexander weeping on the plains of Punjab,
his spearmen muttering and sore,
all the east unveiled and no more worlds to win.
How long could coves hold gray Odysseus
before he fell through doors again,
found himself full-scream again, chasing doubts across the sea?
Achievement almost ends it, but does not.
The fighting outlasts what is fought.
And you, wind chaser, king of cold calls,
I'm tossing you this wreath of words
to wish you blessings that you don't deserve:
that she'll consent to rule your heart
and wait for you where autumn starts;
take your heavy year-scarred hands
and lead you home to quiet lands.

As I Watch You Get Dressed

They'll pay for this. I mean the ones
with the sour faces: the help-desk temps and copier guys;
the privates first class; most driving school instructors;
the old and all the old at heart,
bookkeepers of their own disappointment,
draining their accounts as quick as they can.
Now—today—with the scent of your hair on my belly,
I want to pull the floor up over our heads.
I want this afternoon to loop itself around a vagrant year
like wisteria and maybe it would but it can't.
People out there are checking their phones.
They're shoving hours down stairs,
herding the minutes like guards in a gulag and
soon their thumbs will start to shrivel.
The plants will die. Their shoes will crack. But I
intend to hide inside us. Burn all bridges. Eat the key.
I'll make no sound but the sound of your name and
hope tomorrow loses our home address.
Maybe next week will miss its connecting flight.
Maybe the future will wander like an old man
through the frozen foods as
we feed each other naked oranges, let
the sweet juice trickle
down our chins.

Invention

When you were only three years old,
you'd dress yourself in record time
and stand beside your mother's shoes,
prepared by six for church at nine.

It wasn't doctrine that woke you up.
You never cared much for St. Paul.
You liked to watch the blue stained glass
make winter on a white lace shawl.

At home your dad kept seven geese,
but wouldn't fix the kitchen door.
Your mother searched the couch for change.
They'd argue as you swept the floor.

And you, enmeshed in *Charlotte's Web,*
what drove you to imagine more?
To hold your heart up like a hand,
so sure the world had gifts in store?

Answer this, and I'll explain
how I can praise and yet still be
amazed, amused, and terrified
to think your life could include me.

37

What we need is a post-coital poetry:
cantos for those of us with limited time and even less money
but a surprising number of socks.

It would proceed quietly, so as not to wake the kids.
In our case, this poetry would
understand the way my wife looks with her hair wet.
Know how *I* sound with hay fever, wearing blue slippers,
a cat conformed to my ankles.

This poetry might,
if it is up past ten o'clock, help with the dishes.
It could throw away these brown bananas, pick up
towels off the bathroom floor.

In a locket it would wear
a very small snapshot of us
when we were nineteen years old. Small because
it hurts to see such things again,
to breathe that dangerous air. Because I swear I
now prefer the sound of her in other rooms,
admonishing the toy chest and
because the dog's gone missing again,
off another of his random expeditions,
all smell, all urge, and someone has to
bring him back.

It's Not That I Mind

It's just that I could have been something more
than I've turned out to be—the guy who sits here
perched at the edge of the tub
making Waldo the Whale breech in the bath
once more before the toys go nightnight or
brushing your hair into agreeable furrows, then
wrestling your pajama bottoms on.
It wasn't supposed to be like this. See
before I met your mother and time telescoped into
this endless sequence of average events
I kayaked the green cold waters of the upper Arkansas,
listened at night for the cries of wolves, or worse,
under stars so sharp I put a hat on when I stood.
Now I wrangle rubber ducks. I dole out pastel medicines,
take my usual seat for reading
goodnight mittens, goodnight mush and
watch for monsters till you fall asleep,
your fist a small heart in my hand.
I listen to your breathing flatten out like
a lowland river leaving its banks and realize once again
I could have been something more and now I can't,
in fact I wouldn't if I could if it meant
leaving you behind.

Wish We Were There

I figured our anniversary trip to the beach
would be the perfect chance
for Sara and me to get orgiastically drunk.
We'd shout secrets to the moon again and
talk about things that don't make sense
when we're assembling a table that came in a box.
The kids are six and four now,
old enough to understand what "water slide" means,
so I resolve to leave the laptop home.
By noon we're out of Austin and life is great again
until just south of Seguin the little one starts to vomit.
She soaks herself. Her dress. Her seat.
Sara's sick a few minutes later, so we
introduce ourselves to every Dairy Queen
on the highway headed south.

We make Port A at 8. I unload the truck,
thinking *What does not kill me makes me stronger* but
by midnight I'm a victim too. I drape my shoulders
over the edge of the tub and feel myself dragged inside out.
The weekend's as hopeless as a bug on its back.
We spend days on the couch sipping
room service soup we can't afford
and trying to keep the kids from staining the rug.
All told, our vacation is twenty minutes on the beach.
Not a single Petrarchan sonnet composed.
No chakras awakened. No beer cans scrunched
      beneath our naked flanks.

Back in Austin, we pack tomorrow's tuna fish.
There's a moment, then, when we can either salvage something
from the fact we're here, together, or ignore it.
Write the time off. Try next year.
MoPac's cars sloosh past a block away.

Sara whispers, *Hear that? Hear the waves?* and
curves herself into my stomach like a line of dying surf.
Outside the streetlight blinks to life.
I understand. It's not the moon.
Sometimes you have to improvise.

Managed Care Jesus

I call my wife Managed Care Jesus
because she has for many years
carried the corporate cross,
mended frayed provider networks,
set up a thousand conference calls but
it's more than that in fact
mostly it's our daughters
who urgently need lamotrigine
and a seasonal affective disorder lamp
(what in my day we called the "the sun")
and something to say to the teddy bear boyfriend
who's now an abuser
because he wants what Daughter One won't give
you are only as happy as
your unhappiest child
the wise among us say, whoever they are
and this time they're right
my wife carries all of it inside her
like a drug mule on a long-haul flight
every worry, every insult,
every slight to their teenage egos
and I worry one day
her body will turn to lead or heavier
the weight of all that worry actually
bearing her—*boring* her—downward
into the earth like an augur
until she stands upright
six feet under and I say
sweetheart do you want some coffee
and she says no thanks, not just yet
I have to pay the deposit

Consolations

It's not the things you plan for, pray for,
strangle into being but what
happens anyway, regardless of your own wrong turns:
the laughter of your two-year-old, amazed by her bath, or
that cool night in October when
moonlight drifts so deep in your backyard
you need a shovel to get to the Subaru.
A horned owl hoots behind the garage.
The Buddha was right. Your kids
will learn to drive, make dumb decisions, end up in the papers
or maybe not. Your Dell stock hasn't gained a dime.
You can chase a thing forever, never get it, and
almost fail to see the bridge below the dam is clear.
The trees are standing there, waving you on, and suddenly
Town Lake's a spill of Spanish coins.
Light and shadow. Shadow. Light.
Don't think you're blessed. You're blessed.
Take the treasure you've been given, drive it home and
hope some portion stays inside you.
Hope it starts to burn down deep.

Morning in Jerusalem

Daughter I have no idea
how heaven feels or
if I'll ever be allowed to know
but I would like to think that
some time—many times—I will be myself again
and hear you call me by my favorite name.
I'll grin as I walk into your room
and from the crib you haven't learned to climb from yet
you'll look at me and
raise your arms.

Baz

Her Arab colt is
Baz, which means
the "wild horse of Yemen."
But not yet.
Three months on
we still stop every night
to watch as he
blinks heavily,
drowsy, soft-faced as
a thicket-hidden
fawn.

Cedar shavings
cling to him
like sleep.
Stay down, she says.
He cocks one hoof.

Walking back
through stars as
thick as snow I hear
a rabbit run
a mile away. I breathe
to break my lungs and she
says all of this
is ours.

About the Author

Bruce McCandless lives in Austin, Texas with his wife and two daughters. He has published stories and poems in *Pleaides, The Seattle Review, The Texas Observer,* and *The Asian Wall Street Journal.* Bruce is an avid cyclist and hiker. When he's not reading or writing, he's probably out on the Barton Creek Greenbelt with one (or two) of his dogs. He's currently working on a non-fiction book about NASA and the manned space program called *Wonders All Around.*